By Milan Blue

Disclaimer:

The information and advice presented in this book are solely for informational purposes. The author and the publisher assume no responsibility for any losses or damages that may arise from the application of the information presented in this book. It is the responsibility of the reader to independently assess and determine whether the content and recommendations presented are suitable for their individual situation. Neither the author nor the publisher are liable for any errors or omissions in this book.

Copyright Disclaimer:

This book and all its contents are protected by copyright. All rights, including reproduction, reprinting, electronic or mechanical recording, and distribution of the contents, are reserved. No part of this book may be reproduced or transmitted in any form without the written permission of the author or the publisher. Unauthorized use, reproduction, or distribution may result in civil and criminal penalties. All registered trademarks, trade names, and product names mentioned in this book are the property of their respective owners and are used here for identification purposes only.

Christian Taormina
c/o IP-Management 30479
Ludwig-Erhard-Str. 18
20459 Hamburg

Distraction during Grooming	7
Brushing	11
Bath Time	17
Ticks or other pests	25
Coat Care	33
Hairstyles	39
Hair Trimming	43
Eye	51
Ears	59
Paws	69
Nail	81
Oral and Dental	93

Distraction during Grooming

Grooming your Cocker Spaniel is a vital aspect of their care routine, contributing to their health and hygiene while fostering a strong bond between you and your furry friend. Yet, for some dogs, grooming can be a source of stress, whether due to discomfort, fear of certain tools, or past negative experiences. To ensure grooming sessions are enjoyable for your Cocker Spaniel, various techniques can help soothe and distract them.

Positive reinforcement is a fundamental method to keep your dog relaxed during grooming. Reward them with treats, praise, and gentle petting throughout the process to reinforce good behavior and create a positive association with grooming.

Desensitization is another effective approach. Start slowly with less invasive tasks like gentle brushing and paw touching before progressing to more complex grooming tasks such as nail clipping or bathing. Gradually exposing your Cocker Spaniel to each step can help them feel more comfortable and confident.

The grooming environment plays a crucial role in your dog's comfort. Ensure the grooming area is quiet, relaxing, and comfortably warm. Playing soothing music or using calming essential oils can further enhance the atmosphere and help ease your dog's nerves.

Providing chew bones or toys can also help distract your Cocker Spaniel during grooming. Offering a safe and engaging toy can keep them occupied and focused, reducing their anxiety during the grooming process.

Consider incorporating TTouch massages into your grooming routine. These gentle touches and massage movements, known as Tellington Touch, can help alleviate stress and promote relaxation in your Cocker Spaniel, making grooming a more soothing experience for them.

Above all, pay attention to your dog's body language and respond to their needs accordingly. If they show signs of discomfort or stress, take a break and try again later. Patience and empathy are essential for ensuring grooming sessions are positive and stress-free for your Cocker Spaniel.

Brushing

Regular grooming sessions are essential for the well-being of your Cocker Spaniel, offering a multitude of benefits for their health and appearance. Beyond simply enhancing their looks, there are compelling reasons why dedicating time to brushing your Cocker Spaniel is a valuable investment.

Primarily, brushing aids in the removal of loose hair from your Cocker Spaniel's coat. This is especially crucial for dogs with longer hair, as loose strands can easily tangle and form mats. These mats not only cause discomfort but also pose risks of skin irritations, pain, and potential infections. By brushing regularly, you can effectively prevent matting and ensure your dog's coat remains healthy and lustrous.

Furthermore, brushing stimulates circulation in your Cocker Spaniel's skin and evenly distributes natural oils throughout their coat. These oils play a vital role in maintaining coat health, reducing dryness, and minimizing issues like dandruff. As a result, your dog's skin stays moisturized, smooth, and well-nourished.

To optimize the benefits of brushing, it's crucial to select the appropriate brush for your Cocker Spaniel's coat type and grooming needs.

There are different types of brushes, each suitable for different types of fur and needs:

Undercoat rake: Ideal for dogs with dense undercoats, this brush removes loose hair from the undercoat and prevents matting. It often has dense, rounded bristles that glide gently through the fur without irritating the skin.

Rubber brush: Particularly suitable for dogs with short fur, this brush has soft rubber tips that remove loose hair while massaging the skin to promote circulation.

Slicker brush: This brush has thin, flexible wire bristles and is ideal for dogs with long, curly, or wiry fur. It thoroughly removes mats and knots and helps to detangle the fur without causing damage.

A comb: Useful for smoothing your dog's fur after brushing and ensuring that no mats or knots remain. There are different types of combs, including metal combs with tight teeth for dense fur and soft combs with wide teeth for more sensitive skin.

By choosing the right brush for your dog and regularly grooming its fur, you can not only enhance its appearance but also promote its health and strengthen your bond. Brushing your dog is thus not only a duty but also a valuable opportunity to spend time with your beloved four-legged friend and meet its needs.

When grooming dogs, it is important to consider that different breeds have different types of fur and therefore require specific brushes to maintain their fur optimally. Using the wrong type of brush can cause discomfort to the dog or even damage its fur.

Here's a detailed consideration:

- Short-haired fur that is less prone to matting, yet they should still be brushed regularly to remove loose hair and promote skin health. A rubber bristle brush or glove is ideal for removing loose hair and massaging the skin, which promotes circulation and makes the fur shiny.

- In contrast, long-haired require regular brushing to avoid matting and keep the fur clean and healthy. An undercoat brush or a brush with fine metal bristles works best here to remove loose hair, untangle mats, and detangle the fur without causing damage.

- Dogs with curly or wiry fur also require special care. Their curly hair is prone to matting and requires a brush with flexible bristles or a wire brush to untangle mats and keep the fur shiny without damaging the curls.

- For double-coated a combination brush with bristles and wire pins is ideal. This allows for the removal of loose undercoat, untangling mats, and grooming the fur without damaging the topcoat.

How often should I brush my dog?

The frequency of brushing depends on several factors, including the breed, coat type, season, and your dog's individual needs. Dogs with long hair typically require more frequent brushing, ideally several times a week, to prevent matting and keep the coat healthy. During shedding seasons in spring and autumn, it may be necessary to increase brushing to remove dead hair and promote the growth of new hair. Dogs with short hair may require less frequent brushing, usually once a week, unless they have strong hair growth or skin issues that require additional care.

Are there specific techniques or tips I should consider when brushing my dog?

There are some important techniques to consider when brushing your dog to achieve optimal results. Begin with gentle, even strokes and work your way slowly to brush your dog's entire body. Use the right brush for your dog's coat type and pay attention to areas that are prone to matting, such as the underside of the legs, armpits, and belly. Also, check your dog's skin for signs of irritation, parasites, or other issues while brushing.

Can I brush my dog too much?

Yes, it is possible to brush your dog too much, which can lead to skin irritation, dryness, or even hair loss. It's important to brush in moderation and consider your dog's needs and the condition of their coat. If your dog already suffers from skin problems or has sensitive skin, you should be especially careful not to cause further irritation. If you're unsure how often to brush your dog, consult your veterinarian or a professional groomer for recommendations tailored to your dog's specific needs.

Bath Time

Keeping your Cocker Spaniel's skin healthy is paramount to their overall well-being. Regular baths using a gentle dog shampoo are essential not only for cleansing their coat of dirt and excess oil but also for promoting skin circulation and removing dead skin cells. This regimen aids in maintaining skin health and lowers the risk of skin issues such as inflammation, hot spots, and fungal infections. Furthermore, a healthy coat acts as a natural barrier against parasites, deterring fleas, ticks, and other pests.

Over time, dogs can accumulate unpleasant odors from various sources, including outdoor activities and interactions with other animals. Bathing effectively eliminates these odors and prevents their recurrence by removing dirt and bacteria, which are common odor culprits. A freshly bathed dog not only smells better but also feels more comfortable and revitalized.

Moreover, bath time offers an opportunity for you to conduct a thorough health check on your Cocker Spaniel. While bathing, you can closely examine their skin for any signs of abnormalities such as redness, flaking, or rashes, which may indicate underlying health issues. Additionally, you can check for injuries or swelling that might otherwise go unnoticed. Early detection enables prompt treatment and helps prevent potential complications.

Bathing your Cocker Spaniel involves several key aspects, each contributing to a successful and enjoyable experience.

Here are the key aspects of bathing:

- Before bathing your dog, thorough preparation is crucial. Start by organizing the bathing area. Gather all necessary materials, such as dog shampoo, towels, a brush or comb, and if necessary, a non-slip mat to prevent your dog from slipping. Ensure that the bathing area is warm and safe, and place all utensils within reach to facilitate a smooth process.

- Choosing the right shampoo is crucial for a successful bath. There are a variety of dog shampoos on the market, so it's important to select one that suits your dog's needs. A mild, pH-balanced shampoo specifically designed for dogs is ideal, as it won't irritate the skin and maintains the natural balance of the skin. Depending on your dog's needs, you can also choose specialized shampoos that work against flea or tick infestation or are suitable for sensitive skin. Also consider the scent of the shampoo to ensure it's pleasant for your dog.

- Before applying the shampoo, thoroughly moisten your dog's coat with warm water. This helps loosen dirt and debris and evenly distribute the shampoo. Use a gentle water stream to calm your dog and ensure that the entire coat is well saturated. This step can be particularly important if your dog has long or dense fur, as it can be more difficult to evenly distribute the shampoo when the coat is dry.

- Apply the shampoo evenly to your dog's wet coat and work it in thoroughly. It's best to start at the neck and work your way back. Be sure to avoid the eyes, ears, and nose of your dog, and use a mild shampoo that won't irritate. Gently massage the shampoo into your dog's coat and skin to remove dirt and excess oil and cleanse the skin. A good tip is to apply the shampoo in a foaming motion to ensure it's evenly distributed and reaches all areas of the coat.

- After the shampoo has been thoroughly worked in, it's important to rinse it thoroughly from your dog's coat. Use warm water for this and make sure to remove all residues completely. Inadequate rinsing can lead to skin irritation, so it's important not to neglect this step. Pay special attention to rinsing the shampoo from denser areas of the coat, such as under the legs and between the toes, to avoid irritation.

- After bathing, it's important to thoroughly dry your dog to prevent it from catching a cold or bacteria from multiplying in the damp fur. Use an absorbent towel to remove excess water, then dry your dog's coat with a hair dryer on a low setting. Be sure not to set the hair dryer too hot to avoid burns and keep it at a reasonable distance from your dog's coat to avoid overheating. Start with the larger areas of the coat and then work your way to the smaller areas to ensure that everything is dried evenly. Don't forget to thoroughly dry your dog's ears and paws to prevent infections.

- After bathing, you can comb or brush your dog's coat to remove tangles and smooth it out. This not only promotes a healthy and shiny coat but also helps remove excess hair and promote circulation of the skin. You can also use special grooming products such as conditioner or sprays to care for and protect the coat from environmental influences. Some conditioners can also help detangle the coat and loosen knots, which can be particularly useful if your dog has long or curly fur. After grooming and drying your dog's coat, reward him with a treat or play session to reinforce the positive experience of bathing.

How often should I bathe my dog?

The frequency with which you should bathe your dog depends on various factors, including your dog's individual skin and coat condition, lifestyle, and outdoor activities. Generally, it's recommended to bathe your dog every few months unless there are specific reasons for more frequent bathing, such as heavy soiling or a skin condition requiring regular cleaning. However, excessive bathing can remove your dog's natural oils and lead to skin irritation. It's important to find the right balance to keep your dog's skin and coat clean and healthy without irritating or drying it out.

How can I best acclimate my dog to bathing if he doesn't like it?

If your dog doesn't enjoy bathing, it's important to make the process slow and positive to reduce his fear or discomfort. Start by gradually acclimating your dog to the water, initially familiarizing him with small amounts of water and rewarding him with treats or praise to create positive associations with the bathing area. Use gentle touches and speak in a calm and soothing voice to calm your dog during bathing and provide him with security. It can also be helpful to associate bathing with other enjoyable activities such as playing or walking to make the experience more positive.

What alternatives are there to traditional bathing if my dog doesn't like water?

If your dog doesn't like water or is afraid of bathing, there are some alternative methods for cleaning and grooming his coat. One option is to use dry shampoo or grooming wipes specifically designed for dogs. These products allow you to clean and refresh your dog's coat without immersing him in water. You can apply the dry shampoo to your dog's coat, massage it in, and then wipe off excess product with a towel or brush. Grooming wipes are also convenient for quickly cleaning paws or other areas without needing water. Another option is professional dry cleaning at a dog salon, where special cleaning techniques and products are used to clean your dog's coat without water. If your dog is afraid of water, it's important to be patient and take things slowly to build trust and make the experience enjoyable.

Are there special tips for bathing puppies compared to adult dogs?

Bathing puppies requires special attention and caution as their skin and coat are still sensitive and developing. It's important to use gentle products specifically designed for puppies to avoid irritating or drying out their skin. Start slowly and gradually introduce your puppy to bathing to acclimate them to water and create positive experiences. Avoid submerging your puppy's head underwater or flooding them as this can cause fear or discomfort. Be sure to thoroughly rinse your puppy's coat to remove shampoo residues and gently and completely dry them to prevent chilling.

Ticks or other pests

In the realm of Cocker Spaniel care, dealing with ticks and other parasites is an ongoing concern for dog owners. These tiny yet troublesome pests not only cause discomfort but also pose significant health risks to our cherished furry companions.

Ticks rank among the most prevalent parasites that dogs encounter. These minuscule arachnids latch onto the dog's skin to feed on their blood, potentially transmitting severe diseases such as Lyme disease, anaplasmosis, ehrlichiosis, and babesiosis. These illnesses can manifest in symptoms like fever, lameness, loss of appetite, and in severe cases, life-threatening complications. Hence, it's vital to regularly remove ticks and employ preventive measures like tick repellents to thwart infections.

Fleas are another bothersome adversary for dogs. These diminutive insects not only cause incessant itching and discomfort but can also induce allergic reactions and skin irritations. Flea bites may also transmit tapeworms, posing an added hazard to your dog's well-being. Effective flea control entails a multifaceted approach, including routine combing, sanitation of the dog's living space, and the use of flea prevention products.

Moreover, dogs may fall prey to other pests like lice, mites, and bugs, each capable of inflicting skin irritations, itching, and general discomfort. Lice feed on skin flakes, leading to intense itching and skin irritations. Mites can trigger conditions such as demodicosis and sarcoptic mange, resulting in skin issues and hair loss. Bugs, meanwhile, can cause painful bites and provoke allergic reactions.

Combatting these pests demands a proactive stance and consistent care regimen. This encompasses regular grooming, vigilant monitoring of the coat's condition, routine bathing and brushing, and the application of suitable preventive measures such as flea and tick control products. Additionally, maintaining cleanliness in the dog's surroundings, including their resting area and the outdoor space, is crucial to minimize the risk of infestation.

Here is a more detailed guide on how to check your dog for ticks and other pests:

- Before you begin the inspection, create a calm and relaxed environment for your dog. Find a well-lit area, ideally outdoors or in daylight indoors. Calm your dog by speaking gently to him or petting him to keep him calm during the inspection. Make sure you have all the necessary materials on hand, including a tick removal tool or tweezers, cotton swabs, and disinfectant.

- Start the examination with your dog's head. Thoroughly inspect the ears, the area around the eyes, the muzzle, and the mouth. Look for small black dots or movements that could indicate ticks. Lift the fur gently to check the skin and watch for signs of redness or irritation.

- Continue to examine the rest of your dog's body. Part the fur into sections and carefully inspect the skin underneath. Focus on areas such as the neck, shoulders, back, abdomen, and legs. Particularly in warm and moist areas like the armpits and groin, ticks may like to hide.

- Use your hands to feel your dog's body for any bumps or lumps. Look out for raised or itchy spots that could indicate a flea infestation. Gently massage the skin to uncover any hidden parasites.

- Thoroughly examine your dog's fur for signs of lice or mites. Look out for hair loss, skin irritations, or small black dots that could indicate lice feces. Take your time to check your dog's entire coat and ensure no parasites are overlooked.

- If you discover a tick, carefully grasp it with a tick removal tool or tweezers close to the skin and slowly and evenly pull it out. Be careful not to squeeze the tick's body to minimize the risk of infection. Thoroughly disinfect the bite site with disinfectant to reduce the risk of infection.

- If you notice signs of fleas, lice, or mites, consult your veterinarian for appropriate treatment. Your vet can help you choose an effective flea and tick preventative and take suitable measures to combat other parasites.

- To prevent future infestations, use flea and tick preventatives regularly according to your veterinarian's instructions. Also, be sure to keep your dog's environment clean by washing his bed regularly and cleaning the area around his sleeping area.

Things to avoid when it comes to controlling ticks and other pests in dogs:

- It's important never to remove ticks with bare hands. This can increase the risk of infection as the tick may burst, allowing pathogens to enter the bite site. Using tick removal tools such as tweezers or tick removers is the safest method to remove ticks as they firmly grasp the tick's body and prevent tearing.

- Home remedies or alternative methods for pest control should not be used as the sole solution. Some of these methods may be ineffective or even contain harmful ingredients that could compromise your dog's health. Always consult a veterinarian before trying new treatment methods.

- It's crucial to use flea and tick preventatives according to the manufacturer's instructions and not apply an excessive amount to your dog. Overdosing on preventative products can lead to side effects and jeopardize your dog's health. If you're unsure about how much to use, consult your veterinarian.

- Don't focus solely on treating your dog; remember to also clean and treat his environment. Fleas and ticks can survive in carpets, furniture, and other areas of the house, leading to a re-infestation. Wash your dog's bedding regularly and thoroughly clean the house to eliminate parasites.

- If you notice signs of discomfort, skin irritation, or other symptoms in your dog, don't ignore them. These could be signs of an infection or an underlying condition that requires appropriate treatment. Consult your veterinarian to discuss the best course of action and ensure your dog's health.

How often should I check my dog for ticks and other pests?

The frequency of checking your dog for ticks and other pests depends on various factors, including the location, your dog's outdoor activities, and the season. Generally, it's recommended to check your dog for ticks at least once daily, especially after outdoor walks or time spent in wooded or grassy areas.

Are there specific seasons when the risk of tick infestation is higher?

Yes, the risk of tick infestation is typically higher during the warmer months of the year, especially in spring and summer. Ticks prefer warm and humid climates and are more active during these seasons. However, in some regions, the risk of tick infestation may persist throughout the year, particularly in areas with mild winters. It's important to check your dog for ticks year-round and take appropriate preventive measures to prevent infections.

Coat Care

The coat of a Cocker Spaniel is a captivating and multi-faceted aspect that extends beyond its mere appearance, playing a vital role in their daily lives. Over millennia of evolution, it has adapted to serve various functions, making it an indispensable part of a dog's existence.

In the distant past, the fur of canine ancestors was instrumental for survival. It offered protection against harsh elements like cold, heat, and moisture, aiding in camouflage for hunting and evading predators.

Today, in modern dog life, fur continues to fulfill diverse roles. It acts as a thermostat, storing warmth in winter and repelling heat in summer, crucial for dogs living in varied climates. Additionally, it acts as a shield against UV radiation, dirt, insects, and scratches, safeguarding the delicate skin beneath.

Moreover, fur serves as a medium of communication. Changes in color or texture can convey emotions or health status. For instance, a matted fur might signal stress, while a glossy coat indicates vitality.

Psychologically, fur holds great significance. Grooming fosters a bond between dog and owner, providing comfort and affection. Regular care, including brushing, prevents mats, identifies skin issues early, and ensures a shiny, healthy coat, thus optimizing its natural functions.

By understanding and tending to the needs of their fur, owners can ensure their Cocker Spaniel's coat not only looks its best but also contributes to their overall well-being, enhancing the special bond shared between them.

Coat Type

Dogs can have a variety of coat types, ranging from long and dense to short and wiry. Each coat type requires specific grooming approaches to keep the fur in optimal condition.

Here is an in-depth look at the different coat types:

Single Coat: Some Cocker Spaniels have a single coat, which consists of a dense, smooth layer of fur that lies close to the body. This type of coat is relatively low-maintenance and requires regular brushing to remove loose hair and prevent matting. Single-coated Cocker Spaniels may shed less than their double-coated counterparts, making them a suitable choice for individuals with allergies or those who prefer a cleaner home environment.

Double Coat: Many Cocker Spaniels have a double coat, which consists of a dense, insulating undercoat and a longer, silky outer coat. This double-layered coat provides protection against the elements and may vary in texture and length depending on the individual dog. Double-coated Cocker Spaniels require more frequent grooming to prevent matting and tangles, particularly in areas such as the ears, chest, and tail. Regular brushing and occasional trimming are essential to keep their coat looking neat and healthy.

Curly Coat: Some Cocker Spaniels may have a curly or wavy coat, which adds an extra layer of charm and personality to this already adorable breed. Curly-coated Cocker Spaniels require regular grooming to prevent matting and tangling, as their curly fur can easily become tangled if not properly cared for. Regular brushing and occasional trimming are essential to maintain their curly coat and keep them looking their best.

Straight Coat: While less common, some Cocker Spaniels may have a straight coat that lacks the waves or curls typically associated with the breed. Straight-coated Cocker Spaniels still require regular grooming to keep their fur in good condition, but they may be slightly easier to maintain than their curly or wavy counterparts. Regular brushing and occasional trimming can help keep their coat looking sleek and shiny.

Feathering: Many Cocker Spaniels have feathering on their legs, ears, chest, and tail, which adds to their overall elegance and beauty. Feathering consists of longer, silky hair that adds texture and volume to the coat. While feathering enhances the Cocker Spaniel's appearance, it also requires regular grooming to prevent matting and tangling. Pay special attention to these areas during grooming sessions, using a slicker brush or comb to remove tangles and keep the feathering looking neat and tidy.

The diversity of coat types in dogs is a fascinating example of the adaptability and versatility of these animals. Each coat type has its own advantages and disadvantages, and choosing the right type often depends on various factors, including the dog's lifestyle, the climate it lives in, and the activities it engages in. Regardless of the coat type, proper care is crucial to ensure the dog's health and well-being.

A healthy diet also plays a crucial role in coat care. A balanced diet, rich in high-quality proteins, omega-3 fatty acids, and vitamins, significantly contributes to promoting a healthy coat. Protein-rich foods such as meat, fish, and eggs, as well as omega-3 fatty acids from fish oil, flaxseed oil, and certain nuts, are particularly important.

Hairstyles

Dogs can sport various hairstyles to suit their personality and lifestyle. From the cute and cuddly teddy bear cut to the practical and low-maintenance kennel clip, there's a hairstyle for every pup.

Teddy Cut
The Teddy Cut is a popular grooming style for Cocker Spaniels that gives them a cute and cuddly appearance. This style involves trimming the fur short all over the body, leaving the coat fluffy and uniform in length. The face is trimmed to create a rounded shape, resembling that of a teddy bear. The Teddy Cut is low-maintenance and keeps your Cocker Spaniel looking adorable while minimizing the need for frequent brushing and grooming.

Country Cut
The Country Cut is a versatile grooming style that combines practicality with style. This style involves leaving the body fur slightly longer, while trimming the fur on the face, legs, and tail to a shorter length. The coat is kept neat and tidy, with the longer body fur adding a touch of elegance and flair. The Country Cut is suitable for Cocker Spaniels who enjoy outdoor adventures and want a practical yet fashionable look.

Cupcake Cut

The Cupcake Cut is a fun and whimsical grooming style that adds a touch of sweetness to your Cocker Spaniel's appearance. This style involves trimming the fur short on the body, leaving the coat fluffy and rounded, resembling the shape of a cupcake. The face is trimmed to create a round, cherubic expression, while the ears are left slightly longer to enhance the overall cupcake effect. The Cupcake Cut is perfect for Cocker Spaniels with a playful and outgoing personality who want to stand out from the crowd.

Kennel Cut

The Kennel Cut is a practical grooming style that is often chosen for its simplicity and ease of maintenance. This style involves trimming the fur short all over the body, including the face, legs, and tail. The coat is kept neat and uniform in length, making it easy to groom and care for. The Kennel Cut is ideal for Cocker Spaniels who lead an active lifestyle and need a hairstyle that can withstand the rigors of outdoor adventures.

Experimenting with different dog hairstyles can be a fun way to express your pup's personality and style. Whether you opt for the cute and cuddly teddy bear cut or the practical and low-maintenance kennel clip, grooming your dog's coat with care and attention will keep them looking their best. So, grab your grooming tools and get ready to unleash your dog's inner fashionista with a fabulous new hairstyle!

Hair Trimming

Hair trimming for a Cocker Spaniel is not just about looks; it's a comprehensive grooming practice vital for their overall well-being.

First and foremost, proper trimming is crucial for maintaining skin hygiene and health. Cocker Spaniels have dense fur that can easily trap dirt, allergens, and even parasites like fleas and ticks. These can irritate the skin and lead to infections if not properly addressed. Regular trimming helps to remove excess hair along with any accumulated dirt and debris, keeping the skin clean and reducing the risk of skin issues.

Moreover, Cocker Spaniels are prone to tangling and matting due to their long and silky fur. These tangles not only cause discomfort but can also lead to more severe problems such as skin irritation and even infections. Trimming the fur helps to prevent tangling and matting by maintaining a manageable length and removing any knots or tangles that have formed.

Furthermore, proper trimming plays a crucial role in regulating the dog's body temperature. Cocker Spaniels have a double coat that provides insulation against both cold and heat. However, excessive fur can impede the dog's ability to regulate its body temperature effectively, leading to overheating in warm weather and potential hypothermia in cold conditions. Trimming the fur helps to optimize insulation, ensuring that the dog stays comfortable regardless of the weather.

Finally, grooming and trimming contribute to the overall aesthetics of the Cocker Spaniel. A well-trimmed coat not only enhances the dog's appearance but also reflects their overall health and vitality. It accentuates their natural features and ensures that they look their best at all times.

Some trimming methods for cutting dog hair:

The use of scissors is one of the most common methods for cutting dog hair. Manual scissors or electric clippers with various attachments can be used to trim the hair to the desired length. This method is particularly suitable for dogs with long or dense fur.

Clippers with special shaving heads or blade attachments can be used to cut the hair to a very short length or even shave it. This method is especially suitable for dogs with short fur or for areas that require a smooth shave, such as the belly or paws.

Trimming scissors are special scissors with serrated blades that can be used to evenly trim the hair and cut thinner hairs. They are suitable for trimming facial hair, paws, and other sensitive areas where precise cutting techniques are required.

Thinning scissors have serrated or notched blades that can be used to thin and texture the hair without cutting it too short. This method is suitable for dogs with dense or thick fur to reduce volume and achieve a uniform texture.

Detangling combs or slicker brushes can be used to loosen tangles or mats in the fur before cutting the hair. This is especially important for dogs with long or curly fur to ensure that the hair can be cut evenly and without pulling.

Step by step introduction

- Preparing to trim your dog's hair is key to a successful and stress-free experience. Start by creating a calm and relaxed environment. Play with your dog or do some calming exercises to ensure they are comfortable. Make sure you have all the necessary tools handy, including high-quality dog scissors or clippers, combs or brushes for detangling and smoothing the fur, as well as treats to reward and soothe your dog during trimming.

- Before you begin trimming, it's important that your dog is clean. Thoroughly bathe them with a mild dog shampoo to remove dirt, dandruff, and excess oil. Ensure the fur is completely dry before starting trimming, as damp fur is more difficult to cut and can increase the risk of skin irritation.

- Take time to carefully examine your dog's fur. Look for tangles, knots, parasites, or skin irritations. Gently detangle the fur with a comb or brush and remove any tangles to allow for even trimming. Also, check your dog's skin for signs of irritation or injuries, and address them accordingly before continuing with trimming.

- Choosing the right tools is crucial for successful trimming. Depending on the length, texture, and density of your dog's fur, you may need different tools. Ensure the tools are clean and sharp to ensure smooth and precise trimming.

- Before starting trimming, determine the desired length of the fur. Consider their individual needs, and your personal preferences. If you're unsure which length is best, start with a longer setting and gradually work your way up to achieve the desired length. Keep in mind that the fur will appear shorter after trimming than when it's dry, so be conservative with your cutting lengths.

- Start trimming at the contours of your dog's body, such as the ears, neck, and paws. Use a steady hand and keep your dog calm and secure during trimming. Respect the natural lines of the fur and emphasize the body's shape. Work systematically, cutting the fur in small sections, making sure not to injure your dog's skin. Pay special attention to areas with denser or longer fur, such as the ears or paws, and trim them carefully to achieve a uniform appearance.

- After defining the contours of your dog's body, you can start trimming the body itself. Work systematically, cutting the fur in small sections, ensuring even cuts. Hold the trimmer or scissors at an appropriate angle and work in the direction of hair growth to achieve a smooth and uniform result. Be careful not to cut too deeply to avoid skin irritation, and regularly check if the fur looks even.

- Be especially careful when trimming around sensitive areas such as eyes, nose, ears, and genitals. Use scissors instead of clippers for these areas if necessary to minimize the risk of injuries. Gently pull the skin around these areas if needed to ensure you're cutting the fur safely, and keep your dog calm and secure during trimming.

- After trimming your dog's body, carefully inspect the entire fur for even cuts and correctness. Trim any excess or uneven fur as needed to achieve a clean and groomed appearance. Pay particular attention to areas you may have overlooked during the first pass and correct any irregularities to achieve a professional result.

Regularly reward your dog with treats and praise during trimming to make the experience pleasant and positive. Praise and reward help your dog stay calm and enjoy the process. Take breaks for short breaks in between so your dog can relax, and be patient and empathetic to ensure they are comfortable. Once trimming is complete, thoroughly clean the tools and store them in a safe place.

What are the differences between a dog scissors and a trimmer?

Dog scissors are handheld tools with two blades used to cut your dog's fur. They are particularly useful for precise cuts and trimming sensitive areas such as the paws or face. A trimmer, on the other hand, is an electric tool with rotating blades used to quickly shorten larger areas of fur. Trimmers are ideal for trimming the body or removing longer hairs.

What can I do if my dog is afraid of the trimmer or scissors?

If your dog is afraid of the trimmer or scissors, it's important to be patient and understanding. Start by slowly getting your dog accustomed to the sound and feeling of the trimmer or scissors by initially just placing it near them without touching. Reward them for calm behavior and positive interactions with the tool, and gradually progress by slowly introducing them to trimming.

It's important to note that the exact sizes of trimmer attachments may vary depending on the brand and model. Therefore, it's advisable to check the specific options and sizes of the trimmer you are using.

Eye

Ensuring the well-being of your Cocker Spaniel's eyes is not just about aesthetics; it's a vital aspect of their overall health. The eyes are essential for your dog's perception and interaction with the world around them. To grasp the significance of eye care, it's essential to understand the intricate structure and function of a dog's eyes.

A Cocker Spaniel's eyes are composed of several crucial components, including the cornea, lens, retina, and optic nerve. Each of these elements plays a pivotal role in visual perception and maintaining eye health. The cornea acts as a protective shield and directs light into the eye. The lens focuses incoming light onto the retina, where it is converted into nerve signals and transmitted to the brain via the optic nerve, enabling vision.

Regular eye care routines are essential for preserving the health and functionality of these vital components. By gently cleaning your Cocker Spaniel's eyes, you can eliminate debris such as dirt and dust that may cause irritation or infection.

Moreover, consistent eye care facilitates early detection of potential issues or ailments. Through attentive observation during cleaning sessions, you may identify indicators of redness, swelling, discharge, or changes in pupil size, which could signify an underlying eye condition or health concern. Timely detection is critical, as many eye ailments common in dogs, such as conjunctivitis, corneal injuries, or cataracts, can be effectively managed or treated when identified promptly.

Eye Problems

Dogs can experience a variety of eye problems, ranging from mild irritations to severe conditions. A closer look at the most common eye problems in dogs reveals a variety of causes, symptoms, and treatment options.

- **Conjunctivitis:** This inflammation of the conjunctiva can be caused by infections, allergic reactions, or irritants. Symptoms may include redness, swelling, eye discharge, and increased tear production. Treatment may involve the administration of antibiotics, antiviral or antifungal medications, as well as the application of eye ointments or drops.

- **Corneal injuries:** Scratches, foreign bodies, or injuries can affect the cornea of the eye. This can lead to pain, redness, light sensitivity, and increased tear production. Treatment may involve the use of eye ointments, protective collars, and sometimes even surgical interventions to repair the cornea.

- **Entropion and Ectropion:** Entropion occurs when the eyelid rolls inward, while ectropion describes an outwardly rolled eyelid. Both conditions can lead to irritation, tearing, and infections. Treatment often involves surgical corrections to bring the lid into the proper position and protect the eye surface.

- **Glaucoma:** Glaucoma is a serious eye condition where the pressure inside the eye is elevated, leading to pain, vision loss, and potentially blindness. Treatment may involve a combination of medications, surgical procedures, and regular monitoring by a veterinarian.

- **Cataracts:** Cataracts are clouding of the lens of the eye, which can impair vision. They can be age-related or caused by injuries, diseases, or genetic factors. Treatment may involve the surgical removal of the clouded lens and its replacement with an artificial lens.

- **Cherry Eye (prolapsed nictitating membrane):** This condition occurs when the nictitating membrane protrudes and becomes visible as a pinkish bump. Cherry Eye can lead to irritation, infections, and discomfort. Treatment often requires surgical correction to return the gland to its normal position.

Eye Cleaning

Choosing the right materials for cleaning your dog's eyes is crucial to ensure that the cleaning is effective and does not cause additional problems.

Here are various materials that can be used for cleaning a dog's eyes:

- Soft cloths or cotton pads are gentle on the skin around the eyes and are effective for removing dirt and tear stains.

- Specialized eye cleaners for dogs: These cleaners are specifically formulated to remove dirt, tear stains, and impurities from your dog's eyes without irritating the sensitive eye area. They often contain mild ingredients that are safe for dogs and can help prevent or treat eye problems.

- Prescription eye drops from a veterinarian may be necessary to treat certain eye problems, such as infections or dryness. They can help loosen dirt, fight infections, and improve eye health.

The choice of the right material depends on various factors, including your dog's individual needs, the severity of the dirt, and any existing eye problems.

Regular and careful eye cleaning can help prevent and detect these problems early on.

A Guide to Eye Cleaning:

- When you feel ready to clean your dog's eyes, start by creating a calm and relaxed environment. Nervousness or restlessness can make the cleaning process more difficult, so it's important for your dog to feel comfortable. Use soothing words and gentle touches to relax your dog before starting the cleaning.

- Next, carefully examine your dog's eyes. Look for signs of dirt, tear stains, discoloration, redness, or swelling. Increased tear production may indicate a blockage of the tear ducts, while redness or swelling may be signs of infection or inflammation. If you notice any abnormalities or are unsure, it's advisable to consult a veterinarian immediately.

- To clean your dog's eyes, moisten a clean cloth or cotton pad with the specialized eye cleaner. Begin by gently wiping around the area of the eye to remove dirt and tear stains. Be careful not to make direct contact with your dog's eye to avoid injury.

- It's important to be gentle during the cleaning process and avoid causing unnecessary stress for your dog. Speak soothingly to them and reward them for their patient behavior after cleaning. This way, cleaning becomes a positive experience for your dog and strengthens your bond.

- After cleaning your dog's eyes, gently dab the eye area with a dry cloth to remove excess cleaner or moisture. Be careful not to rub too hard, as this can irritate the sensitive skin around the eyes.

- It is advisable to clean your dog's eyes regularly, especially if they are prone to excessive tearing or if you notice signs of irritation. Regular cleaning can help maintain your dog's eye health and detect problems early on.

When cleaning your dog's eyes, there are some things you should definitely avoid to prevent potential injuries or further problems:

- Never use eye cleaners or eye drops intended for human use. These products may contain ingredients that could be harmful to dogs and may lead to irritation or other health issues.

- Avoid using products containing alcohol to clean your dog's eyes. Alcohol can irritate the sensitive skin around the eyes and cause burns.

- Be careful not to apply excessive pressure to your dog's eye while cleaning it. Too much pressure can cause pain and injure the eye area.

- Do not use rough materials such as paper towels or abrasive fabrics to clean your dog's eyes. These can irritate the sensitive skin around the eyes and cause injuries.

- Never use the same cleaning material for both of your dog's eyes, as this can promote the transfer of germs and infections between the eyes. Use a separate cloth or cotton pad for each eye and dispose of it after use.

- If your dog shows signs of discomfort while you are cleaning their eyes, such as twitching, pulling away, or refusing to keep their eyes open, stop immediately and consult your veterinarian. This could be a sign that the cleaning is uncomfortable or painful.

How often to clean eyes?

Once a week is a good guideline, but adjust the cleaning frequency to your dog's needs and consult your veterinarian if necessary. This helps ensure that your dog can lead a healthy and happy life.

Ears

Understanding the intricate anatomy of a Cocker Spaniel's ears is crucial for their well-being. Ears not only facilitate hearing but also contribute to balance and communication in dogs. To ensure optimal health and prevent potential issues, it's vital to comprehend their structure and provide appropriate care.

A Cocker Spaniel's ears consist of the pinna, or outer ear, which can vary in shape and position—whether upright, hanging, or folded. The pinna plays a pivotal role in collecting and directing sound into the external auditory canal. This canal, a tube-like passage extending from the pinna to the eardrum, is lined with specialized epithelial cells that produce earwax. Earwax acts as a protective barrier, trapping foreign particles and debris.

Regular ear care is paramount to maintaining the health of your Cocker Spaniel's ears. This involves consistent cleaning to remove excess earwax, dirt, and buildup.

Ear Problems

Ear problems in dogs can have a variety of causes, ranging from mild irritations to severe infections or structural anomalies. A dog's ears are a complex system consisting of various parts and can be sensitive to external influences.

Possible Conditions:

- One of the most common ear conditions in dogs is otitis externa, also known as external ear inflammation. This inflammation of the outer ear canal can be caused by various factors, including allergies, moisture, foreign bodies, or infections with bacteria or yeast. Symptoms of otitis externa can vary, but often include redness, swelling, itching, unpleasant odor, discharge, and pain. In some cases, the inflammation can be so severe that the dog's ear appears externally deformed or swollen.

- Ear mites, known as Otodectes cynotis, are another common problem in dogs. These tiny parasites can live in the dog's external ear canal and cause intense irritation. Symptoms of an ear mite infection often include intense scratching, head shaking, and dark deposits in the ear. Ear mites are highly contagious and can easily spread from an infected dog to another, so it's important to isolate infected dogs and treat all dogs in the household.

- Yeast infections are another common cause of ear problems in dogs, especially in dogs with allergies or other underlying health issues.

Excessive yeast growth in the external ear canal can lead to inflammation, which manifests as redness, swelling, itching, and sometimes an unpleasant odor.

- Bacterial infections can also lead to ear problems, especially when the ear is already irritated or injured. Bacterial infections often occur as secondary infections and can cause additional symptoms such as discharge and fever.

- Additionally, ear traumas such as injuries to the external ear canal from scratching, bumps, or other traumas can occur. These injuries can lead to pain, bleeding, swelling, and potentially deformities of the ear.

- In some cases, tumors or polyps may also occur in a dog's ear, causing discomfort and, in severe cases, even hearing loss. Symptoms may vary depending on the location and size of the tumor or polyp.

The treatment of ear problems in dogs depends on the underlying cause and may include antibiotics, antifungals, ear cleaning, ear medications, or in severe cases, surgical interventions.

It is important to consult a veterinarian immediately if there is suspicion of ear problems to receive an accurate diagnosis and appropriate treatment. Untreated ear problems can lead to serious complications and affect the well-being of your dog.

Ear Cleaning

For cleaning your dog's ears, you'll need a set of specific materials that help to perform the cleaning process effectively and safely. Good preparation is crucial to ensure that you have everything on hand to thoroughly and gently clean your dog's ears.

Here are various materials that can be used for cleaning dogs' ears:

- First and foremost, you'll need a special ear cleaning solution designed specifically for dogs. This solution is formulated to remove dirt, wax, and excess oil from your dog's ears without irritating the sensitive skin. You can find these solutions at most pet stores or online.

- Additionally, you'll need sterile cotton swabs or gauze swabs to gently remove dirt and wax from the outer ear canal. Ensure that the cotton swabs or gauze swabs are sterile to avoid potential contamination.

- Furthermore, cotton pads or soft cloths are necessary to remove excess cleaning solution and dirt from the outer ear flap and surrounding skin. These should be soft and gentle enough to avoid irritating your dog's sensitive skin.

- It's also advisable to use disposable gloves, especially if you're sensitive to earwax or cleaning solutions. This can help protect your hands during the cleaning process and prevent potential contamination, especially if your dog already suffers from an ear infection.

- Finally, rewards in the form of treats or affection can be a positive reinforcement during the cleaning process, helping your dog enjoy the experience and remain calm.

A guide to ear cleaning:

- Before you begin the actual cleaning process, carefully inspect your dog's ears. Look for signs of redness, swelling, discharge, or unusual odor. These could indicate an underlying infection or inflammation. If you notice such signs or are unsure whether to clean the ears, it is advisable to consult your veterinarian for appropriate treatment.

- Once you're ready to clean your dog's ears, apply a few drops of the ear cleaning solution to the surface of the ear. Gently massage the base of the ear to distribute the solution and loosen any buildup. The gentle massage also helps promote blood circulation and increase your dog's comfort during the cleaning process.

- Next, use a cotton swab or gauze swab to gently remove dirt, wax, and excess cleaning solution from the outer ear canal. Be careful not to insert too deeply into the ear canal to avoid injury. Use each cotton swab or gauze swab only once to prevent potential spread of germs.

- After removing the buildup, gently clean the outer ear and surrounding skin with a clean cotton pad to remove excess solution. Make sure to hold your dog gently but firmly throughout the process to calm them and effectively perform the cleaning.

- It's important to praise and reward your dog after the cleaning process to show them that they behaved well. Ear cleaning should be integrated into your dog's regular care routine but should not be performed excessively, as this can disrupt the natural balance in the ear canal.

By regularly cleaning your dog's ears and monitoring for any changes, you contribute to ensuring they have healthy and happy ears. If you're unsure or notice any issues, don't hesitate to seek advice from your veterinarian. This way, you can ensure you're providing the best care for your beloved four-legged friend's ears.

The Ear Anatomy

On this page, you will find a depiction of a dog's Ear, illuminating the diverse functions it serves and its contribution to the overall performance of the dog.

Ear movements serve as a means of communication between dogs and their human companions. For example, forward-facing ears can signal attention or interest, while ears flattened against the head may indicate fear or submission.

Dog ears are sensitive and enable them to detect sounds from a distance, allowing them to recognize potential dangers early and react to the presence of prey or other animals.

Dogs can use their ears to locate sounds and better orient themselves. This ability allows them to identify the source of a noise or become more aware of their surroundings.

Ears can help regulate a dog's body temperature by dissipating excess heat. Dogs may shake their ears or prick them up when hot to release heat and prevent overheating.

Ears can also convey a dog's emotions. For instance, erect or forward-facing ears may indicate joy or attentiveness, while ears laid back or flattened against the head can signify fear, aggression, or stress.

How often should I clean my dog's ears?

Generally, it's recommended to clean your dog's ears about once a month unless there's a specific issue that requires more frequent cleaning.

Can I clean my puppy's ears, and if so, at what age should I start?

Yes, you can clean your puppy's ears, but it's important to be particularly gentle and considerate of the puppy's needs. It's advisable to start cleaning the ears as soon as your puppy is old enough to feel comfortable being touched, typically around 8 weeks of age.

Should I clean my dog's ears before or after bathing?

It's often a good idea to clean your dog's ears after bathing, especially if you're allowing water to enter your dog's ears during bathing. Bathing can leave moisture and dirt in the ear canal, which promotes earwax buildup and increases the risk of ear problems. Cleaning the ears after bathing can help remove excess water and dirt to reduce the risk of infections.

Paws

The paws of a Cocker Spaniel are vital for their mobility and sensory perception, making paw care a top priority for dog owners. These furry appendages not only provide stability and balance but also relay essential information about their environment. Thus, maintaining paw health is crucial for their overall well-being.

Healthy paws enable dogs to move freely and comfortably, whether walking, running, or jumping. Injuries or damage to the paws can cause pain and discomfort, impacting the dog's quality of life. Factors such as environmental conditions, physical activity, and genetics can influence paw health.

To ensure optimal paw health, dog owners should regularly perform paw care. This includes cleaning the paws after outdoor excursions to remove dirt, bacteria, and potential contaminants. It's also essential to inspect the paws for signs of injury, cuts, cracks, or inflammation.

Nutrition plays a significant role in paw health, with a balanced diet providing essential nutrients like vitamins, minerals, and omega-3 fatty acids to support skin and paw health. Additionally, choosing suitable surfaces for activities such as walking or hiking helps prevent paw strain and injuries.

Monitoring for warning signs of paw problems is crucial. Lameness, excessive licking or chewing of the paws, redness, swelling, or injuries should prompt immediate veterinary attention to prevent complications and ensure timely treatment.

Paw Problems:

The paws of dogs are susceptible to a variety of diseases and injuries that can affect their well-being and quality of life. From infections to chronic conditions, paw problems can have various causes and often require careful treatment and care from dog owners and veterinarians.

One of the most common diseases affecting the paws of dogs is infections. These can be caused by bacteria, fungi, or viruses and can lead to symptoms such as redness, swelling, itching, pain, and even pus formation. Common infections include bacterial infections like interdigital pyoderma (inflammation between the toes), fungal infections like dermatitis, or viral diseases like papillomavirus. Treating such infections typically requires careful cleaning and disinfection of the affected areas and administration of antibiotics, antifungals, or other medications, depending on the type of infection.

Another common issue is paw injuries. These can be caused by sharp objects, rough surfaces, burns, cuts, scrapes, or foreign bodies and can result in pain, bleeding, swelling, and infection. Treating paw injuries often requires thorough cleaning of the wound, removal of foreign objects and debris, and, if necessary, veterinary care, which may involve suturing or prescribing medication to promote healing and prevent infection.

In addition to acute injuries, dogs can also suffer from chronic conditions affecting the paws. These include diseases such as allergic dermatitis, autoimmune conditions like lupus erythematosus, tumors, or warts affecting paw tissue. Treating such chronic conditions often requires comprehensive diagnosis by a veterinarian and long-term treatment, which may include medication, special diets, physical therapy, or even surgical interventions to alleviate symptoms and slow the progression of the disease.

Furthermore, some systemic diseases can also affect the paws. These include conditions such as diabetes mellitus, thyroid disorders, or kidney diseases, which can lead to skin problems affecting the paws. Treating such conditions often requires comprehensive medical care to manage the underlying condition and prevent secondary complications.

To maintain the health of their dogs' paws, it is important for owners to regularly monitor for signs of problems, keep their paws clean and dry, protect them from injuries, and seek veterinary help when needed. By carefully caring for their furry friends' paws and being attentive to potential issues, dog owners can help ensure that their dogs lead healthy and happy lives.

Paw Cleaning Products:

Here is a detailed list of materials for cleaning dogs' paws and their functions:

Cotton swabs or cotton balls: They are useful for removing dirt and debris between the toes and in the crevices where larger cleaning tools may not be as easily accessible.

Wet wipes: Wet wipes formulated specifically for dog paw care can be used to remove dirt and debris from the paw surfaces. They often contain gentle cleansers and soothing ingredients to care for the skin.

Mild shampoo: A mild, hypoallergenic dog shampoo can be used to remove stubborn dirt and debris from the paws. It's important to choose a shampoo that has been specifically developed for dogs.

Bucket or bowl of warm water: Warm water can be used to clean the paws and loosen dirt. However, care should be taken to ensure that the water is not too hot to avoid burns.

Towels: For drying the paws after cleaning. It's important to thoroughly dry the paws to remove moisture and reduce the risk of skin irritation.

Dog brush or comb: A soft dog brush or comb can be used to remove loose hair, dirt, and debris from the paw surfaces and promote blood circulation in the skin.

Paw balm or paw cream: Specialized paw balms or creams can be used to moisturize and protect the skin of the paws, especially for dry or cracked paws. They often contain moisturizing and soothing ingredients such as shea butter, coconut oil, or aloe vera.

Disinfectant: A mild disinfectant can be used to clean any cuts or wounds on the paws and reduce the risk of infection.

Paw Cleaning:
Here is a detailed guide to caring for dog paws:

- Carefully examine your dog's paws for signs of injuries, cuts, tears, abrasions, swelling, infections, or foreign objects such as thorns or splinters. Also, look out for signs of dryness or cracks in the skin. If you notice any issues, it's important to seek veterinary help immediately.

- Start by cleaning the paw surfaces using a damp cloth or wet wipes to remove dirt, debris, and contaminants from the paws. Pay special attention to the spaces between the toes and in the crevices where dirt can easily accumulate. Be sure to apply gentle pressure and avoid irritating the skin.

- Use a damp cloth or wet wipes to remove dirt and debris between your dog's toes. Be thorough, as moisture and dirt in this area can lead to skin irritation and infections.
- Thoroughly dry your dog's paws with a clean towel to remove excess moisture and reduce the risk of skin irritation. Be sure to pat dry between the toes as well.
- Apply a small amount of paw balm or cream to your dog's paws if needed to moisturize and protect the skin, especially if the paws are dry or cracked. Gently massage the paws to evenly distribute the product.
- For cuts, tears, or other injuries to the paws, you can use a mild disinfectant to clean the wound and reduce the risk of infection. Apply the disinfectant carefully to the affected areas and allow it to dry.

As a dog owner, there are some things you should definitely avoid when caring for your dog's paws. Here are some key points:

- Pay attention to warning signs such as lameness, excessive licking or chewing of the paws, redness, swelling, or signs of pain. These may indicate problems with your dog's paws that should not be ignored.

- A balanced diet is important for your dog's paw health. Do not neglect your dog's diet, as deficiencies in essential nutrients such as vitamins, minerals, and fatty acids can lead to skin problems and poor paw health.

How often should I clean my dog's paws?

The frequency of paw cleaning depends on various factors such as your dog's activity level, environmental conditions, and the condition of the paws. Generally, it is advisable to clean the paws after outdoor walks or as needed. Ideally, once a day.

How can I protect my dog's paws in winter?

In winter, your dog's paws can be stressed by cold, snow, ice, and road salt. Use special paw balms or creams to moisturize and protect the paws, and rinse the paws thoroughly after outdoor walks to remove road salt.

How can I help prevent my dog's paws from becoming dry or cracked?

Regularly moisturizing the paws with a paw balm or cream, as well as using moist wipes or wet wipes to clean and hydrate the skin, can help prevent dry or cracked paws.

Can I clean my dog's paws too often?

Yes, cleaning your dog's paws too frequently can dry out the skin and cause irritation. Clean the paws only as needed and use mild, moisturizing products to nourish and protect the skin.

What role does exercise play in my dog's paw health?

Regular exercise is important for your dog's overall health and well-being, including paw health. Exercise promotes circulation and strengthens muscles, helping to keep the paws healthy and strong.

The Paw Anatomy

On this page, you will find a depiction of a dog's paw, illuminating the diverse functions it serves and its contribution to the overall performance of the dog.

A dog's claws are attached to the ends of the toes and serve various purposes, including gripping surfaces, digging, and defending. Regular trimming of the claws is important to prevent overgrowth and ensure the dog's comfort.

A dog's paw consists of several toes, which can vary depending on the breed. Most dogs have four main toes and a so-called "Dew Claw," a small rudimentary toe located higher on the inside of the front leg.

Unlike humans, dogs do not sweat through their skin but through the sweat glands on their paws. They primarily regulate their body temperature through panting, but sweat on the paws can also help dissipate excess heat, especially on hot surfaces.

Between the toes and the pads are the pads, soft tissue cushions that provide additional cushioning and improve the dog's traction. These pads may be more pronounced depending on the dog's activity and the surface it is on.

The underside of a dog's paw is covered with thick, elastic pads that provide shock absorption while walking. These pads are resistant to various surfaces and help the dog move safely on different terrain.

Each toe is equipped with a toe pad that helps distribute pressure evenly while walking and provides the dog with additional stability. These pads absorb shocks and help protect the joints, especially during jumps or rapid changes of direction.

Should I put shoes or socks on my dog to protect its paws?

In certain situations, shoes or socks can help protect your dog's paws from injuries or weather conditions, especially in extreme temperatures, sharp surfaces, or chemical substances. Make sure the shoes or socks fit properly and are comfortable for your dog.

Nail

The nails of a Cocker Spaniel are essential for their movement, grip, and paw protection, making nail care a priority for dog owners. Healthy nails contribute to the overall well-being of dogs and should be regularly monitored and cared for.

Ideally, a dog's nails should be clean and well-maintained, neither too long nor too short. Overly long nails can hinder walking and cause paw misalignment, while excessively short nails can injure the sensitive tissue underneath, leading to pain and infections.

Regular nail care is vital, involving trimming or filing the nails to an appropriate length. Dog owners should learn proper nail trimming techniques to prevent injuries. If unsure or if the dog is uncomfortable, seeking assistance from a professional groomer or veterinarian is advisable.

In addition to trimming, it's essential to be vigilant for signs of nail problems. Changes in color or texture, cracks, breaks, or signs of infection like redness, swelling, or discharge may indicate underlying health issues. Consulting a veterinarian for diagnosis and treatment is recommended in such cases.

A dog's nails can also reflect their overall health. Brittle nails, for instance, may signal malnutrition or other health concerns. Providing a balanced diet rich in essential nutrients such as biotin, zinc, and omega-3 fatty acids can promote nail health and overall well-being.

Nail Products:

Here is a detailed list of materials for cleaning dogs' nails and their functions:

- Nail clipper: A tool for trimming dogs' nails. There are various types of nail clippers, including guillotine-style, scissor-style, and grinder tools. They allow dog owners to safely and effectively shorten their pet's nails.

- Nail file: Useful for smoothing and shaping the nails after trimming. It can help remove sharp edges and reduce the risk of splinters or tears.

- Some nail clippers are equipped with a safety guard to prevent cutting too much nail at once. This can help prevent injuries and safely trim the dog's nails.

- Nail grinder: An electric tool used to trim and shape dogs' nails. It works by grinding the nails instead of cutting them and can be particularly useful for dogs afraid of clipping or with very hard nails.

- Styptic powder: Used to stop bleeding that may occur when nails are cut too short and the blood vessel in the nail is injured. It often contains ingredients like aluminum sulfate or diatomaceous earth, which help stop bleeding and seal the wound.

- Towel or cloth: Useful for holding the dog during nail trimming and catching excess blood or cleaning solutions.

- Disinfectant: Used to clean and disinfect tools such as nail clippers and files to reduce the risk of infections.

- Treats or rewards: Can be used to reward the dog during the trimming process and promote cooperation. Positive reinforcement can help make nail trimming a positive experience for the dog.

- Flashlight or other light source: Can be helpful for identifying the blood vessel in the dog's nail and avoiding cutting it during trimming.

Nail Problems:

Various diseases and issues can manifest in the nails of dogs. A common problem is ingrown nails, which can lead to pain, inflammation, and infections. Nail injuries such as cuts, tears, or fractures are also common and can result in bleeding and infections.

Nail infections are another challenge that can be caused by bacteria, fungi, or other microorganisms. These infections can lead to inflammation, swelling, and discoloration of the nails. Brittle nails may indicate malnutrition, hormonal issues, or other underlying health problems.

Nail dystrophy, an abnormal change in the structure and shape of the nails, as well as nail tumors and autoimmune diseases, can also cause issues and affect nail health.

To ensure the health of their dog's nails, dog owners should regularly check their pet's nails and watch for signs of problems. Prompt treatment is important to avoid complications and maintain nail health.

As a responsible dog owner, there are some things you should definitely avoid when it comes to caring for your dog's nails. Here are some key points:

- Do not cut your dog's nails too short. This can lead to injuring the blood vessel in the nail (the "quick"), resulting in pain, bleeding, and infections. Make sure to trim only the tips of the nails and avoid the quick.

- Avoid applying excessive pressure on the nails when cutting them. This can cause injuries and increase the risk of breaks or tears. Trim the nails with gentle pressure and in small increments to minimize the risk of injury.

- Never use unsuitable tools for cutting your dog's nails. Nail clippers or files that are not intended for dogs can cause injuries or damage to the nails. Invest in high-quality grooming tools specifically designed for dogs.

- Do not neglect your dog's nails just because they are anxious or restless. It is important to remain patient and calm and give the dog time to get used to the grooming process. Positive reinforcement and rewards can help make the experience more pleasant.

- Do not ignore your dog's nails if you notice issues such as injuries, infections, or other abnormalities. Timely treatment is important to avoid complications and maintain nail health. Consult a veterinarian if necessary.

Trimming Nails:
- Make sure you have all the necessary tools on hand, including nail clippers or a nail file, styptic powder (if needed), disinfectant, and treats for reward.

- Choose a quiet time when your dog is relaxed. Avoid cutting the nails when your dog is excited or restless, as this can lead to injuries.

- Select a well-lit area with enough space to move around. A non-slip surface can help your dog feel secure.

- Allow your dog to become familiar with and smell the tools to reduce fear. Gently touch his paws to get him accustomed to the feeling.

- Be sure to identify the quick in your dog's nail. On light-colored nails, the quick is visible as a pink area, while it's harder to see on dark-colored nails. Shine a flashlight on the nail if necessary to make the quick more visible.

- Hold your dog's paw gently and use the nail clippers to trim the nails carefully. Make sure to cut only the tip of the nail to avoid the quick. Trim small sections at a time and regularly check the progress.

- If necessary, use a nail file to smooth sharp edges and reduce the risk of splits or breaks. File the nails gently into a rounded shape.

- If you accidentally cut the quick and there is bleeding, stop the bleeding with styptic powder and apply gentle pressure to the wound to stop the bleeding. Clean the wound carefully with disinfectant.

- Praise your dog and give him treats as a reward for his cooperation. Positive reinforcement can help make nail trimming a positive experience for your dog.

How often should my dog's nails be trimmed?

Generally, nails should be checked every 2-4 weeks and trimmed as needed.

How do I know when my dog's nails are too long?

Long nails can affect walking and lead to injuries. Watch for nails extending beyond the paw and touching the ground. If you hear a clicking sound when your dog walks on hard surfaces, the nails are likely too long.

Can my dog get nail fungus?

Yes, dogs can develop nail fungus infections, which can cause thickening, discoloration, and detachment of the nails. Timely treatment is important to prevent the spread of the infection.

Can I trim my dog's nails myself or should I consult a veterinarian?

Many dog owners trim their dog's nails themselves, but if you feel unsure or your dog is very anxious, it may be advisable to seek help from a veterinarian or professional groomer.

Are there special precautions for trimming nails in puppies?

Caution is needed with puppies as their nails are more sensitive. Use tools specifically designed for puppies and trim the nails gently to avoid injuries.

Should I trim my dog's nails after bathing or before?

Your dog's nails are softer after bathing, which can make trimming easier. However, you can also trim them before bathing if your dog tends to be restless.

How to Trim Dog Nails

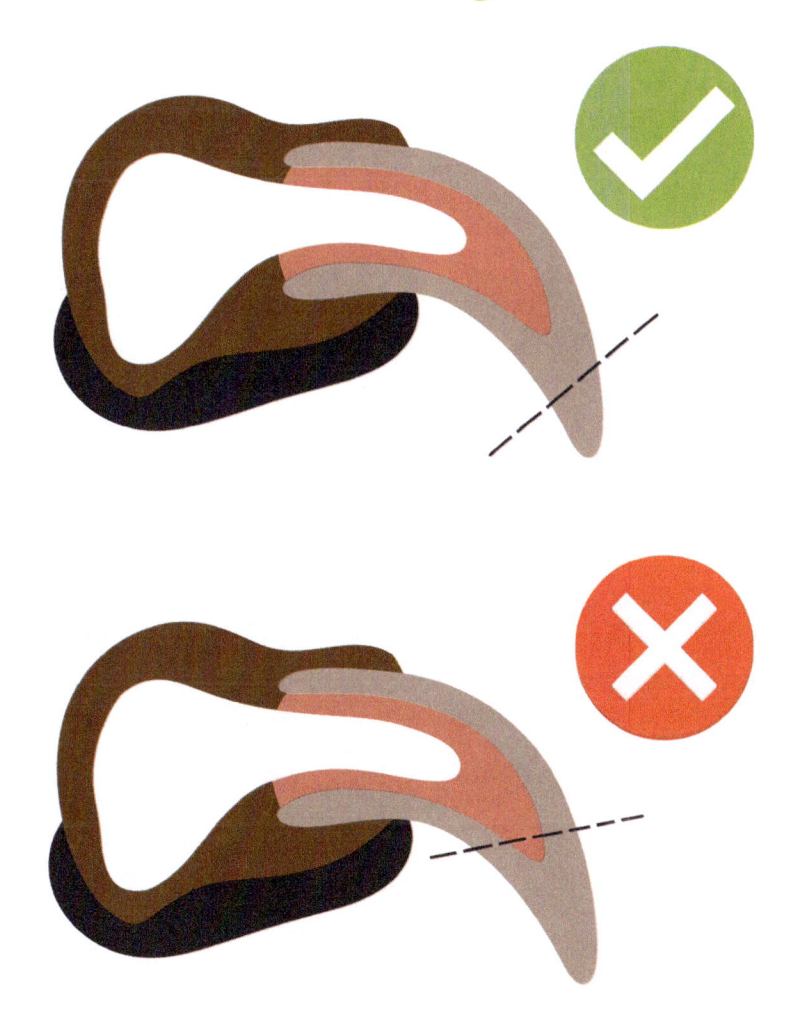

Can I trim my dog's nails only with a nail file instead of cutting them?

Yes, you can trim your dog's nails with a nail file, especially if he is afraid of cutting or has very sensitive nails. However, it may take longer to achieve the desired length.

Oral and Dental

Maintaining oral health in Cocker Spaniels is paramount for their overall well-being and happiness. Like humans, dental issues can significantly impact a dog's health, making regular monitoring of their oral health essential.

Regular brushing with dog-specific toothbrushes and toothpaste is key to reducing plaque and tartar buildup. Additionally, providing appropriate chew toys and treats can aid in cleaning teeth and strengthening gums.

Failure to address plaque buildup can lead to the formation of tartar, which not only affects the appearance of teeth but also contributes to gum inflammation and potential tooth loss. Hence, routine dental cleanings by a veterinarian are often necessary to remove tartar and preserve oral health.

Gum inflammation, a common issue in dogs, can escalate to tooth loss if not promptly addressed. Prioritizing dental care and scheduling regular check-ups with the veterinarian can help prevent or manage gum inflammation effectively.

Persistent bad breath may indicate underlying oral health issues that require attention. Rather than masking the odor, it's crucial to identify and address the root cause through proper dental care and veterinary guidance.

By consistently implementing dental care routines and attending veterinary check-ups, many oral health issues in Cocker Spaniels can be prevented or managed effectively. Optimal oral health not only contributes to their physical well-being but also enhances their behavior and overall quality of life.

Oral Problems:

The oral health of dogs can be affected by various diseases and problems, which not only compromise the well-being of the dog but can also have serious implications for its overall health.

Tartar buildup and plaque accumulation are common among dogs and, if not regularly removed, can lead to tartar, which in turn can cause gum inflammation and tooth loss. These issues can be exacerbated by inadequate dental care, genetic predisposition, or an unbalanced diet.

Gingivitis and periodontitis are other common problems caused by plaque buildup, leading to gum inflammation and more serious gum diseases. These conditions can not only be painful but also affect the tooth-supporting apparatus and result in tooth loss.

Dental abscesses can occur when bacteria invade the tooth, causing an infection. They often require dental treatment to save or remove the tooth and can be very painful.

Dental fractures are common injuries that can be caused by accidents, traumatic events, or chewing on hard objects. Depending on the severity of the fracture, dental treatment may be necessary to repair or remove the tooth.

While oral tumors are less common, they can still occur and cause various symptoms such as swelling, sores, or bleeding. The diagnosis and treatment of oral tumors often require collaboration between a veterinarian and a specialized veterinary dentist.

Timely detection and treatment of oral diseases and problems are crucial for maintaining the oral health of dogs. Regular dental care at home and veterinary check-ups can help identify and treat problems early. Good oral health is not only important for the well-being of the dog but can also help reduce the risk of serious health problems related to the oral cavity.

Oral Products:

Here is a detailed list of materials for cleaning dogs' teeth and mouth, along with their functions:

Dog toothbrush: Specifically designed toothbrush for dogs, featuring soft bristles to avoid gum damage while removing plaque and food debris from the teeth.

Dog toothpaste: Special toothpaste for dogs, available in various flavors and safe for ingestion. They often contain enzymes or ingredients to help dissolve plaque and prevent tartar buildup.

Finger toothbrush: An alternative toothbrush that fits over the finger and is suitable for cleaning the teeth of small dogs or dogs with sensitive gums.

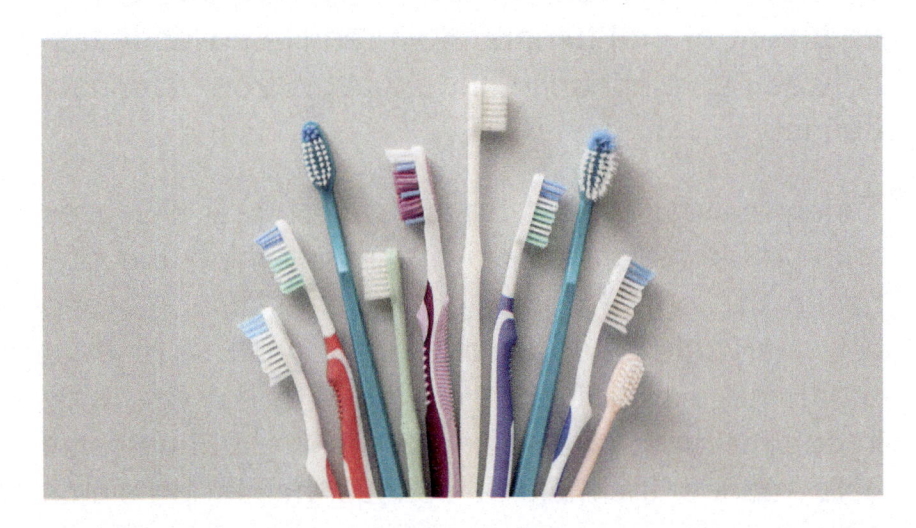

Dental cleaning spray: A spray applied to the dog's teeth and gums to loosen plaque and freshen breath. It can be a good addition to dental care, especially if the dog does not tolerate tooth brushing.

Dog dental chews and toys: Specially designed dental chews and toys that can help remove plaque and massage the gums. They can also help combat boredom and support the dog's natural chewing behavior.

Gum massager: Some special dog toothbrushes feature silicone bristles or nubs that massage the gums and promote circulation. This can help improve oral health and prevent gum disease.

Dental care treats: Special treats for dogs that can help reduce plaque and support oral health. They are often enriched with ingredients that clean and strengthen the teeth.

Mouth health water additives: Some products contain special additives that can be added to the dog's drinking water to promote oral health. These can help dissolve plaque and combat bad breath.

Oral Cleaning:
- Prepare yourself and your dog for dental care by creating a calm and relaxed environment. Make sure you have enough time and that both you and your dog are relaxed before starting the cleaning.

- Gradually introduce your dog to dental care, especially if they have never had their teeth brushed before. Let them smell the toothbrush and toothpaste and lick a bit of the toothpaste to get used to it.

- Place your dog in a comfortable position, either sitting or lying down. You can lay them on the floor, hold them in your lap, or position them on an elevated surface, whichever works best for both of you.

- Gently lift your dog's lips and brush their teeth in circular motions. It's best to start with the canine teeth and then work your way to the molars. Focus particularly on the outer surfaces of the teeth, as plaque tends to accumulate there.

- Gently massage your dog's gums with the toothbrush or your finger. This promotes blood circulation and contributes to the gum's health.

- Praise and reward your dog after each successful dental care session. This helps them develop positive associations with tooth brushing and makes the experience more enjoyable.

- Ideally, perform dental care daily or at least several times a week to achieve optimal results. The more regularly you brush your dog's teeth, the healthier their teeth will remain.

- Pay attention to changes in your dog's mouth, such as tartar buildup, gum inflammation, or bad breath. If you notice anything unusual, consult your veterinarian for advice.

- Regularly have your dog's teeth checked by the veterinarian, ideally during annual check-ups. The vet can detect and treat potential problems early before they lead to serious health issues.

As a dog owner, there are certain things you should definitely avoid when it comes to your dog's dental care. Here are some important points to keep in mind:

- Never use toothpaste for humans to brush your dog's teeth. These often contain ingredients like fluoride that can be toxic to dogs. Instead, use special toothpaste for dogs that can be safely swallowed.

- Avoid using rough or hard toothbrushes that could injure your dog's gums. Instead, choose a toothbrush with soft bristles specifically designed for dogs.

- Avoid applying too much pressure to your dog's teeth, as this can cause gum injuries. Use gentle, circular motions and be particularly careful when working around sensitive areas like the gums.

- Never force your dog aggressively to have their teeth brushed. This can lead to stress and anxiety and strain the relationship between you and your dog. Instead, be patient and give your dog time to get used to dental care.

- Do not use sharp objects such as knives or other tools to remove plaque or tartar. This can cause injuries and harm your dog's gums. Always have dental cleaning performed by a professional.

- Never neglect your dog's dental care. Inadequate dental care can lead to serious oral health problems, including tartar buildup, gum inflammation, and tooth loss. Regularly care for your dog's teeth to maintain their oral health.

- Never ignore signs of problems in your dog's mouth, such as tartar buildup, gum inflammation, or bad breath. These can indicate serious oral health problems that need to be addressed. Seek veterinary advice promptly to recognize and treat potential issues.

Diet for Oral Health

A balanced diet plays a crucial role in your dog's oral and dental health. To properly care for its teeth and mouth, there are some important aspects to consider:

Choosing high-quality dog food that contains all the necessary nutrients to support your dog's health is essential. Look for a balanced mix of proteins, carbohydrates, fats, vitamins, and minerals.

In addition to standard nutrition, you can look for dog food specifically designed to promote dental health. Some types of food contain special ingredients such as crushed bones, fibers, or enzymes that can help reduce plaque and improve oral health.

Supplementing your dog's diet, you can give it chew bones or special dental care toys that massage the gums and help remove plaque.

It's important to avoid sugary treats, as sugar can promote plaque formation. Instead, choose healthy and dental-friendly treats that contain little or no sugar.

You can also use water additives that can help promote your dog's oral health by reducing plaque and combating bad breath.

Make sure your dog drinks enough water to maintain good oral hygiene. Drinking water helps remove food particles and rinse the mouth, contributing to reducing plaque buildup.

Chew Items for Oral Health

Chew items are specially designed products meant to clean and strengthen your dog's teeth and gums. They come in various shapes and sizes, including chew bones, chew toys, chew sticks, and more. These chew items offer numerous benefits for your dog's oral and dental health:

Chewing on chew items can help remove dental plaque and tartar from your dog's teeth. The mechanical action of chewing helps loosen deposits and keep the teeth clean. This helps reduce the formation of dental calculus and lowers the risk of gum disease.

Chewing on chew items also massages your dog's gums, promoting blood circulation and helping to keep the gums healthy. Improved blood circulation can reduce inflammation and support the healing of gum problems.

The intense chewing on chew items can help strengthen your dog's jaw muscles. This is especially important for young dogs that are still growing, as well as for older dogs whose jaw muscles may be weakened.

Chewing on chew items can have a calming and stress-relieving effect on dogs. It also helps combat boredom and prevent unwanted chewing on furniture or other items.

Chew items can be an important supplement to regular dental care, especially if your dog does not tolerate tooth brushing. They provide a simple and effective way to support your dog's oral and dental health without requiring active intervention on your part.

When purchasing chew items, however, there are some important things to consider:

- Choose chew items that are suitable for your dog's size and chewing behavior.

- Make sure that the chew items are made of high-quality and safe materials that do not splinter or pose a choking hazard.

- Avoid chew items with added sugars or additives, as these can affect your dog's oral health.

- Monitor your dog's chewing on chew items and remove them if they become worn out or damaged to minimize the risk of choking.

How often should my dog get chew items to promote his dental health?

Ideally, your dog should have the opportunity to chew on chew items daily to support oral and dental health. However, the use of chew items should be considered as a supplement to regular dental care and not as a substitute for it.

Can poor dental hygiene in my dog lead to behavioral problems?

Yes, pain or discomfort due to dental issues can lead to behavioral changes such as aggression or loss of appetite.

Dog Breed Books

At the End, remember that it's just the beginning of a broader exploration.
We hope you are happy with this book.
The satisfaction of our readers is our priority and we would be happy if you could give us your feedback on the book. It would therefore be great if you would take a moment to write a customer review on Amazon. It only takes you a few seconds. By doing this, you will help other readers on Amazon make better purchasing decisions. Thank you!"

★ ★ ★ ★ ★

SCAN ME

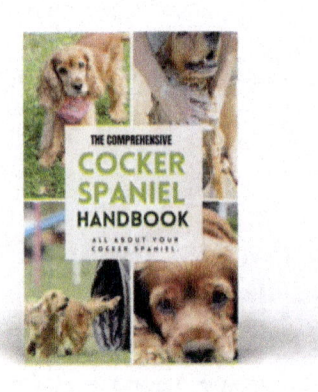

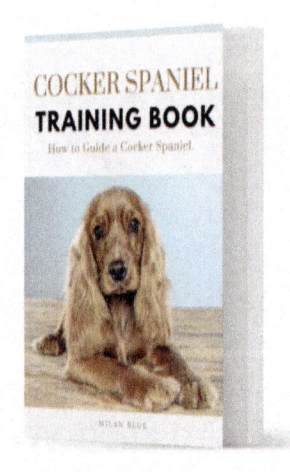

Cocker Spaniel Handbook

$49,99

Purchase on Amazon

Cocker Spaniel Training Book

$29,99

Purchase on Amazon

Printed in Great Britain
by Amazon